Sea Otters

FIRST EDITION

Series Editor Deborah Lock; **US Senior Editor** Shannon Beatty; **Editor** Arpita Nath;
Senior Art Editor Ann Cannings; **Project Art Editor** Tanvi Nathyal;
Picture Researcher Sumedha Chopra; **Production Editors** Christine Ni;
Senior Producer, Pre-Production Nikoleta Parasaki; **DTP Designers** Vijay Kandwal, Dheeraj Singh;
Jacket Designer Charlotte Jennings; **Managing Editor** Soma Chowdhury;
Managing Art Editor Ahlawat Gunjan; **Art Director** Martin Wilson;
Reading Consultant Linda Gambrell PhD

THIS EDITION

Editorial Management by Oriel Square
Produced for DK by WonderLab Group LLC
Jennifer Emmett, Erica Green, Kate Hale, *Founders*

Editors Grace Hill Smith, Libby Romero, Michaela Weglinski;
Photography Editors Kelley Miller, Annette Kiesow, Nicole DiMella;
Managing Editor Rachel Houghton; **Designers** Project Design Company; **Researcher** Michelle Harris;
Copy Editor Lori Merritt; **Indexer** Connie Binder; **Proofreader** Larry Shea;
Reading Specialist Dr. Jennifer Albro; **Curriculum Specialist** Elaine Larson

Published in the United States by DK Publishing
1745 Broadway, 20th Floor, New York, NY 10019

Copyright © 2023 Dorling Kindersley Limited
DK, a Division of Penguin Random House LLC
23 24 25 26 10 9 8 7 6 5 4 3 2 1
001-333921-June/2023

A catalog record for this book
is available from the Library of Congress.
HC ISBN: 978-0-7440-7244-0
PB ISBN: 978-0-7440-7245-7

DK books are available at special discounts when purchased in bulk for sales promotions, premiums, fundraising, or educational use. For details, contact: DK Publishing Special Markets,
1745 Broadway, 20th Floor, New York, NY 10019
SpecialSales@dk.com

Printed and bound in China

The publisher would like to thank the following for their kind permission to reproduce their images:
a=above; c=center; b=below; l=left; r=right; t=top; b/g=background

Alamy Stock Photo: DanitaDelimont.com / Cathy & Gordon Illg / Jaynes Gallery 11ca, Dembinsky Photo Associates / Dominique Braud 4-5; BluePlanetArchive.com: Doc White 16-17; **Dreamstime.com:** Jean Edouard Rozey 18-19; **Getty Images:** Moment / Alan Vernon 21tr; **Getty Images / iStock:** GomezDavid 22c, Toprawman 19cr; **naturepl.com:** Ingo Arndt 7tr, Danny Green 6-7, Michio Hoshino 26-27, Doc White 13, 30cl, 32br, Norbert Wu 14-15, 30cla; **Shutterstock.com:** nvphoto 9tc, rbrown10 8-9, Santiparp Wattanaporn 12cb; **SuperStock:** Mary Evans Picture Library / Pat Leeson 20-21

Cover images: *Front and Spine:* **Dreamstime.com:** Dvoriankin; **Shutterstock.com:** Laura Hedien b, Rimma R cra; *Back:* **123RF.com:** hatza clb; **Dreamstime.com:** Natalia Chernyshova cra
All other images © Dorling Kindersley
For more information see: www.dkimages.com

For the curious
www.dk.com

Sea Otters

Contents

Life at Sea

These are sea otters.
They spend most of
their lives in the water.

Relaxing

They can float on their backs.

Grooming

Their fur keeps them
warm and dry.
They brush their fur
and roll over
to keep clean.

fur

Swimming

Sea otters use their webbed feet and flat tails to swim.

webbed foot

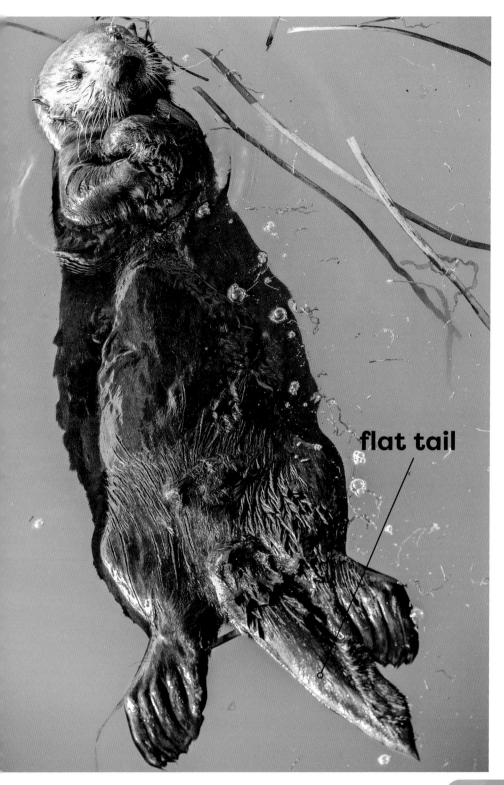

flat tail

Diving

They swim around
to find food.
They dive in and
out of the kelp.

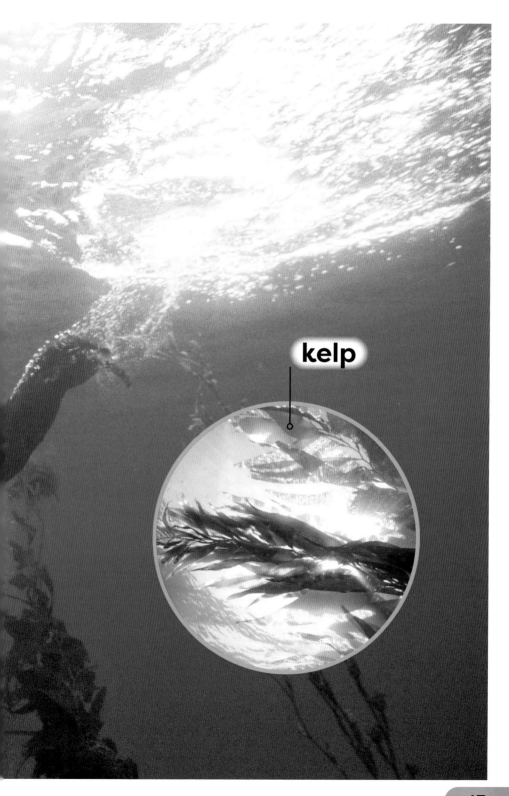

kelp

Hunting

Sea otters hunt for food on the seafloor. They use their whiskers to find food.

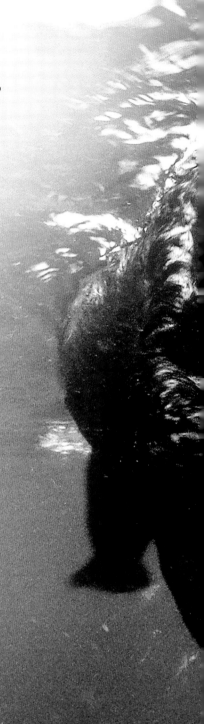

whiskers

Eating

They grab food with their strong paws. Sea otters like to eat shellfish.

shellfish

These are animals with shells, like crabs and clams.

Sea otters hit shells
with stones.
The stones crack
the shellfish open.

They have strong teeth
to bite into their food.

teeth

Caring

Otter pups can only float to begin with. Their moms take care of them.

Sleeping

Sea otters love to rest in big groups.

A group of resting sea otters is called a raft.

Sea otters may wrap kelp around their bodies when they sleep.

The kelp keeps them from floating away!

Glossary

fur
soft hair covering the skin of some animals

kelp
large seaweed with a long stalk

shellfish
a sea animal that has a shell

webbed
fingers or toes joined with a piece of skin

whiskers
long hair growing on the face of some animals

Index

Quiz

Answer the questions to see what you have learned. Check your answers with an adult.

1. Where do sea otters spend most of their lives?

2. What body parts help a sea otter swim?

3. What do sea otters eat?

4. How do sea otters open their food?

5. How does kelp keep sea otters safe?

1. In the water 2. A flat tail and webbed feet 3. Shellfish
4. They hit a shell with a stone until it cracks open 5. It keeps them from floating away when they sleep